THE BIKE SNOB JOURNAL

BIKE SNOB NYC

CHRONICLE BOOKS

SAN FRANCISCO

INTRODUCTION

CYCLING. Like that freaky monolith in *2001: A Space Odyssey*, it is immersive, and it contains all things. What is more beautiful than a Tour de France peloton snaking its way through the Alps? What is more practical and egalitarian than thousands of Dutch bicyclists blithely disregarding the rain during an Amsterdam rush hour? And what image is more disturbing than a recumbent cyclist in sandals with bunions the size and texture of armadillos?

But whether it's beguiling you, or repulsing you, or simply transporting you to work, cycling is always a means of gaining insight into our selves, and a perfect metaphor for life.

If you ride a bike, you probably have lots of containers—a bottle for your water, a saddlebag for your tools, panniers for your personal possessions, and maybe even a foam bucket for your brain. Think of this journal as a container for your thoughts, a vessel into which you can pour your observations concerning the vicissitudes of velocipeding. Instead of Facebooking, or Tweeting, or, worst of all, blogging about your ride, put pen to paper and write about it the old-fashioned way instead. Express the joy you felt as you crested that climb. Keep a log of that bike tour. Or just vent by describing in graphic detail all the things you'd like to do with a pair of tweezers to that asshole in the SUV. (Just don't let the police get their hands on it or they might use it as evidence.)

To help coax all this out of you, I've included various inspirational thoughts, observations, reflections, quotations, pieces of advice, and bits of lore throughout this journal. Some are related to racing, some are related to commuting, and some are simply about riding. Some are edifying, and some are idiotic. Some are drawn from my blog, others are culled from my books, and still others just came to me while I was riding around town in a chicken suit.

Also, to further assist you in your process of self-discovery, this journal contains a small handful of "activities," though actual participation in these activities is completely optional.

So lean your bike against a tree, stretch out on a grassy hillside, take that box of crayons out of your handlebar bag, and start scribbling. Above all, both cycling and writing lead to happiness, and when you combine the two the effect is synergistic. That's certainly been my experience. Immerse yourself in your love of cycling, let the words come, and with any luck you'll push on through to the point where your love of cycling meets your love of life.

Ride safe and write recklessly,

BIKE SNOB NYC

Everything about riding a bicycle compels
you toward beauty.

> "It is by riding a bicycle that you learn the contours of a country best, since you have to sweat up the hills and coast down them. Thus you remember them as they actually are, while in a motor car only a high hill impresses you, and you have no such accurate remembrance of country you have driven through as you gain by riding a bicycle."
>
> —ERNEST HEMINGWAY

> "Give a man a fish and feed him for a day. Teach a man to fish and feed him for a lifetime. Teach a man to cycle and he will realize fishing is stupid and boring."
>
> —DESMOND TUTU

IN BICYCLE RACING AS IN LIFE, there is a fine line between ambition and delusion. The former is the fuel for success, and the latter is the way to ruin. So settle down, pick a wheel to follow, and stay out of trouble.

THE KEY to urban commuting is using the right tool for the job. In the city a bike is a scalpel, and a car is a pair of lefty scissors.

"As a child growing up in pre-gentrification Boerum Hill, Brooklyn, I went everywhere by bicycle. My bike was in many ways the key to my neighborhood, which, at the time, was Boerum Hill, Brooklyn. This was in the '60s and '70s, before all the white people and restaurants. I really can't underscore boldly enough the fact that I grew up in Boerum Hill, Brooklyn, before it was gentrified. You could get mugged!"

—JONATHAN LETHEM

IN A ROAD RACE, always avoid breakaways. Leaving the pack and joining a breakaway is like going from a cushy job at a big company with a regular paycheck to a really hard job at a start-up company where you have to work sixteen-hour days on commission only and people are always yelling at you.

EXCUSES are far more important than equipment. Put the carbon wheels on eBay, but never squander your inventory of excuses.

CYCLING IS SELF-EXPLANATORY, and it will reveal itself to you as you ride. Get a bike—any bike—and the rest will follow.

HI, COMMUTING CYCLIST! Welcome to the United States. You're on your own. Now strap on your helmet and pretend you're a car.

SAVING THE EARTH is a shaky reason for commuting by bike. You know what's even more "green" than cycling? Rollerblading. Think about it.

If polystyrene takes
hundreds of years to
biodegrade, how come
we're supposed to
replace our helmets
every three years?

BICYCLES are the only vehicles that don't come with lights. The law requires all new bikes come with crappy reflectors and fork dropout tabs, yet lights are considered an aftermarket item.

TO RACERS, any time spent on the bike that is not either racing or training for racing is considered "junk miles." To everyone else, racing and training for racing is considered "going nowhere fast."

COMMON SENSE DICTATES that any ride from which you don't return with beer is "junk miles."

ALWAYS LUBE YOUR CHAIN. Your bicycle is an elegant and efficient form of transport. It should not sound like a nest of hungry sparrow chicks.

LOOK BEHIND YOU before launching a "snot rocket," "loogie," or any similar phlegm- or mucus-based projectile. The next cyclist to take a hunk of lung cheese to the face could be you.

TWO THOUSAND YEARS AGO Archimedes famously said, "Give me a large enough lever and a place to stand and I will move the world!" Well, nobody ever gave him that lever, and that's why the world is still in pretty much the same place now as it was then: between Venus and Mars, orbiting the sun, and crawling with idiots.

TELLING CYCLISTS to get out of the road is like telling women to get out of the voting booth and go back into the kitchen, or telling Japanese-American people to "Go back to China!" The ignorance inherent in the statement is almost more offensive than the sentiment behind it.

GREAT TWENTY-FIRST-CENTURY
ANTI-VELOIST DOUCHEBAGS

"I don't take my car and ride on the sidewalk
because I understand that's not for my car.
Why do these people think that these roads
were built for bicycles? . . . . and so you tap
them. I'm not saying you kill them. I'm saying
you tap them. Tap them once . . . pop them a
little bit and see what happens."

—ESPN RADIO HOST TONY KORNHEISER

"And what I compare bike lanes to is swim-
ming with the sharks. Sooner or later you're
going to get bitten . . . My heart bleeds for them
when I hear someone gets killed, but it's their
own fault at the end of the day."

—ROB FORD, MAYOR OF TORONTO

"When I become mayor, you know what I'm
going to spend my first year doing? I'm going
to have a bunch of ribbon-cuttings tearing out
your fucking bike lanes."

—FORMER CONGRESSMAN ANTHONY WEINER
(forced to resign after Tweeting pictures
of his genitals)

IN THE NINETEENTH CENTURY, people hated bikes because they scared the horses. Now they hate them because they think they get in the way of the cars.

SALMON [v]: To ride the wrong way against traffic. *There I was, salmoning along Eighth Avenue, and the next thing I know I'm covered in sticky brown liquid.*

BIKE SALMON [n]: One who salmons. *The next bike salmon I see is getting a venti Frappuccino in the face.*

THANKS TO THE POPULARITY of compression socks, the only difference between bike racers and nursing home residents is that the nursing home residents have social lives.

THE FIXED-GEAR TREND is a natural response to roadie excess. After all, state-of-the-art carbon fiber road racing bicycles with complicated gear-changing systems can cost thousands of dollars, whereas fixed-gear bicycles with handmade frames, top-end parts, and colorful wheels and tires cost just a few thousand dollars.

"DON'T BUY UPGRADES, RIDE UP GRADES," said Eddy Merckx, whose top-of-the-line bicycle frame retails for $6,000.

WHEN YOU RIDE A BIKE your errands can be as enjoyable as your recreation. A bicycle is a tool that turns drudgery into joy.

THE ONLY REAL DEFENSE against bike theft is having a crappy bike. "Fancy" and "city bike" are not compatible. When a fancy bike gets stolen, you are gutted. When a real city bike gets stolen, the thief is practically doing you a favor.

AMERICAN BIKE COMMUTER CHECKLIST:

- ☐ $200 technical pants that are just at home on the bike as they are in the boardroom
- ☐ Matching $200 merino hoodie
- ☐ $500 SPD-compatible kangaroo leather wingtips
- ☐ $3,500 exquisitely lugged steel commuter bike
- ☐ $100 hand-tooled leather carrying strap
- ☐ $300 hand-sewn backpack
- ☐ Delusion that you are somehow saving money by commuting by bike

DUTCH BIKE COMMUTER CHECKLIST:

☐   Bike

WHY ARE OFFICE SHOWERS considered an amenity? Getting naked at work is much more awkward and uncomfortable than being dirty at work.

"If my career were a hairstyle, it would be helmet-head."
—ANDY GARCIA

ARGUABLY, the bicycle industry is more robust than the automobile industry. This is partly because it is smaller and more nimble in the same way a bicycle is smaller and more nimble than a car, but it's also because the simple fact is that lots of people ride bikes. Either way, Trek has never asked for a government bailout.

YOUR COMMUTE IS NOT A COMPETITION.
When commuter races commuter, the only
winner is disgrace.

"Consider a man riding a bicycle. Whoever he is, we can say three things about him. We know he got on the bicycle and started to move. We know that at some point he will stop and get off. Most important of all, we know that if at any point between the beginning and the end of his journey he stops moving and does not get off the bicycle he will fall off it. That is a metaphor for the journey through life of any living thing, and I think of any society of living things."

—WILLIAM GOLDING

CYCLING doesn't have to be about who you know and what you ride. It's about who you are and that you ride.

WHY DO WE HAVE SUCH A HARD TIME RIDING BICYCLES? We now look at our pornography on computers more powerful than the ones that sent Apollo 11 to the moon, yet the typical adult is completely confounded by the humble bike. Give an American a supercomputer and he'll know exactly what to do (look at porn), but give him a bicycle and he'll either strap a couple of cameras to his head and try his best to die, or else he'll hide it in the garage like it's some kind of cursed monkey's paw.

AMSTERDAM is what Portland could be like in five hundred years when it finally gets over itself.

RELIGION AND FIXED-GEAR CYCLING have a lot in common. Both involve following lots of rules that don't really make much sense, and few people are able to engage in either unless there are other people around to watch.

IF WINNING IS TOO HARD FOR YOU, simply race "pass/fail." This means finishing=passing and getting dropped=failing. Riding for the win means you'll probably lose. However, if you treat simply finishing the race as success, you can strive for—and attain—something close to perfection.

CHASING AN ATTACK? Leave that to someone else. An attack is like an ex who tries to "friend" you on a social networking site—you don't follow it, you just ignore it and hope that it goes away.

David Byrne does not own a car.

LIKE IT OR NOT, pedestrians are always right.

SHOAL [v]: When cyclists stop in front of one another at a red light instead of queuing up behind, thus blocking the crosswalk and protruding out into traffic like a shoal, or sandbar. Shoaling *is an incredibly rude practice, and it's tantamount to cutting in front of someone at an ATM, supermarket checkout, or urinal.*

SANDBAR OF IDIOCY [n]: A formation of shoaling cyclists.
Because she refused to shoal, she had to pick her way through the Sandbar of Idiocy *after the light turned green.*

WHEN YOU SPOT A STRANDED CYCLIST on the side of the road, always ask if they need help, but never slow down enough to hear the reply.

UPGRADES ARE USELESS. There's no piece of equipment you can buy that will make you a better cyclist—the exception being that, if you've been riding without a saddle, installing one will do wonders.

DRINK BEFORE YOU'RE THIRSTY AND EAT BEFORE YOU'RE HUNGRY. Also, get dropped before the big climb and not on it; it's a lot easier to ride back to the car that way.

WHEN YOU GET LAPPED in a cyclocross race, it's like you're an Alka-Seltzer and the race is a big glass of water, and everybody gets to watch your effervescent, frothy demise.

CYCLOCROSS is like *Pet Sounds* by the Beach Boys. You're supposed to pretend you like it, even if you don't understand the appeal.

IF ALL ELSE FAILS, comfort yourself with your superiority over the other riders in areas outside of racing. Sure, the guy who passed you just then was stronger than you, but there's no way he's better at cooking eggs than you. You're the Egg Master.

YOUR RACING SHOULD ALWAYS BE TRAINING FOR OTHER RACING.
Road season is preparation for cross season; cross season is for fitness in the off-season; mountain bike racing is to improve bike-handling for road and cross season. If you're doing it right, you're in a constant state of preparation so you never have to succeed at any of it.

"I'm the paté on the universal cracker. I'm the grout holding your shower tiles on. I'm out of the saddle, sprinting up that hill and eating glazed donut bracelets off the right arm of Jesus."

—CHARLES MANSON

UNICYCLING would have a lot more street cred if people called it "humpin' the pizza cutter."

Bike lanes are the tributaries of a beautiful future.

JOOP ZOETEMELK ONCE SAID, "The Tour de France is won in bed," failing to add that it's often lost in the laboratory once they've analyzed the pee-pee samples.

FIVE HANDY EXCUSES FOR THAT POSITIVE DRUG TEST RESULT:

☐ "I am a chimeric twin."

☐ "A spectator spiked my *bidon*."

☐ "I ate tainted meat on the rest day."

☐ "I'm not cheating but the other guy is, so some of his urine must have splashed into my cup during the collection process."

☐ "I inhaled secondhand marijuana smoke while doing intervals in the vicinity of a drumming circle."

☐ "I just *reeeally* wanted to win that charity ride."

MESSENGER LEGEND tells of a golden age when the fax machine was their only competition, email didn't exist, and mighty herds of couriers roamed the city, plentiful and free like tattooed buffalo.

EVERYBODY wants to look like a bike messenger yet nobody wants to look like a food delivery cyclist. I guess you're just not cool if your package is delicious.

LOOSE TOE CLIPS are the hanging-down suspenders of the twenty-first century.

IN PORTLAND, every month is Bike Month, every other head is dreadlocked, and the people are simple but the beer is crafty.

"Perhaps the most vivid recollection of my youth is that of the local wheelmen, led by my father, stopping at our home to eat pone, sip mint juleps, and flog the field hands. This more than anything cultivated my life-long aversion to bicycles."

—TENNESSEE WILLIAMS

"Perhaps the most vivid recollection of my youth is that of being flogged by the local wheelmen, along with the field hands, the postman, and a young Tennessee Williams. This more than anything cultivated my life-long aversion to his plays."

—TRUMAN CAPOTE

HELMETS ARE LIKE YARMULKES: their biggest benefit is that they make wearers feel good about themselves. Using your brain is even more important than putting foam around it.

TRAFFIC RULES weren't made to be broken. However, they were made for cars, which is mostly the same thing.

> "I came out for exercise, gentle exercise, and to notice the scenery and to botanise. And no sooner do I get on that accursed machine than off I go hammer and tongs; I never look to right or left, never notice a flower, never see a view—get hot, juicy, red—like a grilled chop. Get me on that machine and I have to go. I go scorching along the road, and cursing aloud at myself for doing it."
>
> —H.G. WELLS

Q: How many bikes is too many?

A: It varies from person to person, but if you're contemplating a second monstercross bike then you're just about there.

COMPONENT UPGRADING spreads like a disease. You put a new part on your bike, then the part next to it looks crappy, so you've got to replace that one as well. Before you know if you've replaced every single part on the bike, but it's still the same bike you had before, only a lot more expensive.

RIDING WITH A POWER METER is like having sex with an electrocardiograph: it takes the fun out of the whole enterprise and buffets you with data you don't really need. Physical sensation will guide you through your ride the same way it guides you through sex, and if you can't do either without electronics it's possible you have a problem that technology by itself may be insufficient to address.

IT'S EASY to fall into the myth of your own awesomeness, so I find it helpful to remind myself once in a while that we all suck at riding bikes, and that the one of us who sucks the least wins the Tour de France.

> "When I see an adult on a bicycle, I do not despair for the future of the human race."
>
> —H.G. WELLS

ROADIES are like the Amish, or like Hasidic Jews. You might not want to be one, but it's good to know they're there being extremely uptight for the rest of us.

TRIATHLETES are the turduckens of the cycling world.

KNOWING WHAT YOU LOVE is knowing yourself, and something that you love can serve as a guide. It's a fixed and tangible point in the world on which you can pin your passions and hopes. You can have a relationship with cycling. You can enjoy the discipline of cycling, or the freedom; you can enjoy the physical exertion, or the convenience and relative ease. Regardless, a strong relationship based on love will take you far, and it will also improve other areas of your life. You can depend on cycling in a way you can depend on little else.

A FRIEND is someone who will screen your helmet cam footage and edit out all the red lights you ran while you're recovering in the hospital.

IF YOUR BICYCLE IS MAKING NOISE, take the time to diagnose the problem. If you're not prepared to take the week off work to figure out what's making that strange ticking sound then perhaps bicycle ownership is not for you.

THE BIKE is far less important than the ride. Focusing entirely on the bike is like picking a university based on how comfortable the chairs in the lecture hall are.

MODERN ROADS were built for bicycles, not cars. We were here first.

RETROGROUCH [n]: Lover of lo-tech parts and high-spoke-count wheels who always dwells approximately fifteen to twenty years in the past and who uses only components that have proven themselves over long periods of time. Can be found astride steel bicycles with lugs and resplendent in wool garments, or behind Linux computers writing screeds about marketing gimmickry.

The retrogrouch's beard bristled with distaste as the rider on the carbon fiber frame passed him.

FRED [n]: Consumer of any product that promises increased performance. Possesses a tendency to monitor data obsessively and often displays a riding ability inverse to the cost of his equipment. Can be found astride pro team replica bicycles and resplendent in pro team jerseys from completely different teams. Has a strong attraction to carbon fiber.

The Fred scoffed at the bearded man on the steel bike as he overtook him on his state-of-the-art Team RadioShack Trek Madone.

HIGHLY SPURIOUS FRAME MATERIAL PRIMER

What stuff do they make bikes out of and what's the difference between them? Here's an introductory guide so you too can spout nonsense on Internet bike forums:

STEEL

who rides it: Retrogrouches, singlespeeders, people with beards

benefits: Comfortable, durable, repairable

drawbacks: Causes owners to drone on about how their frames are comfortable, durable, and repairable

ride quality: Like sitting on a bed of warm peat

TITANIUM

who rides it: People who bought them used from the people who originally bought them back in the '90s, when they were weapons-grade exotica billed as "the last bike you'll ever buy"

benefits: Durable, which means you don't have to replace them

drawbacks: Durable, which means you don't have an excuse to replace them. May also be radioactive as the cheaper ones were made from spent nuclear fuel rods

ride quality: Like being held aloft in a leather armchair while dancing the hora at a bar mitzvah

ALUMINUM

who rides it: Racers on a budget

benefits: Light, inexpensive

drawbacks: Listening to people with steel and titanium bikes insisting your perfectly good bike rides like a jackhammer

ride quality: Like being held aloft in a metal folding chair while dancing the hora at a bar mitzvah

CARBON FIBER

who rides it: Racers, Freds, people who subscribe to *Bicycling* magazine

benefits: It's what the pros ride; it's light; exotic frame shapes provide lots of room for branding

drawbacks: Expensive, will be dated faster than your iPhone, can't be recycled, environmentally unfriendly manufacturing process kills endangered marine life, baby seals, and kittens

ride quality: Laterally stiff, vertically compliant, and longitudinally paradoxical

BAMBOO

who rides it: People with even longer beards than the people who ride steel bikes, people who build their own bongs

benefits: Sustainable, gives you major smugness points

drawbacks: Bikes look like the raft Tom Hanks lashed together in *Castaway*, may attract hungry pandas

ride quality: Like sitting in a patio furniture display at Pier 1 Imports

WOOD

who rides it: Lumberjacks, furniture enthusiasts, people in Portland

benefits: Prettier than bamboo bikes and you can knock on them for luck

drawbacks: Flammable, may attract termites

ride quality: Just think of the lyrics to "Rock-a-Bye Baby" and you've got the idea

THE BIKE SNOB QUIZ SECTION!

WHAT'S MY SMUGNESS?

CYCLISTS—even the most humble among us—can be a little, well, smug. Whether it's reminding your colleagues that you rode your bike to work, sporting a "One Less Car" tattoo on your forehead, or just heading down to the local greenmarket on your bakfiets, chances are that on some level you know that riding a bike makes you that much better than the rest of humanity. But how smug are you? Take this simple test to find out:

1) When people ask you if you have a car, which best matches your response?

   ☐ Yes (0 POINTS)

   ☐ Technically yes, but I never drive it (2 POINTS)

   ☐ Does a VW Microbus that runs on canola oil count as a car? (3 POINTS)

   ☐ How dare you. Cars are the whale meat of the twenty-first century. (100 POINTS)

2) A bicycle is not truly practical unless:

   ☐ It has brakes (0 POINTS)

   ☐ It has fenders and racks (2 POINTS)

   ☐ It can carry a week's worth of groceries for a family of four (3 POINTS)

   ☐ It can carry your VW Microbus when it runs out of canola oil (1,000 POINTS)

3) How many times have you moved residences by bike?

   ☐ Never (0 POINTS)

   ☐ Once (2 POINTS)

   ☐ More than once (3 POINTS)

   ☐ Is it technically "moving by bike" if I live in my bakfiets? (1,000 POINTS)

4) What is your typical cycling footwear?

☐ Clipless cycling shoes (**0 POINTS**)

☐ Casual shoes/sneakers (**2 POINTS**)

☐ Handmade artisanal locally grown sustainable organic sandals (**3 POINTS**)

☐ I don't require shoes due to my formidable calluses (**STOP COUNTING, YOU HAVE ATTAINED SMUGNESS TRANSCENDENCE**)

WHAT'S MY SMUGNESS RESULTS:

0–2 POINTS: Negligibly smug

4–8 POINTS: Slightly smug

9–12 POINTS: Welcome to Portland

100+: Off the charts, and probably off the grid

HOW EPIC WAS MY RIDE?

SOMETIMES a simple bike ride isn't enough and you crave a bike adventure—you know, one that feels like a spiritual journey and makes you totally useless at work the next day. Rides like this are often called "epic," but the word "epic" is used so liberally now it's hard to know how truly epic your ride was. Here's a detailed scoring system to help you quantify it:

1) Distance

☐ Give yourself one point for every mile

☐ Give yourself double points for each mile that was unpaved

☐ Give yourself triple points for every yard of molten lava you forded

2) Conditions

Was it:

☐ Hot? (1 POINT FOR EVERY DEGREE OVER 80)

☐ Cold? (2 POINTS FOR EVERY DEGREE UNDER 40)

☐ Raining steadily? (10 POINTS)

☐ Snowing heavily? (3 POINTS FOR EVERY INCH OF ACCUMULATION)

☐ Hailing? (10 POINTS FOR EVERY MINUTE YOU REMAINED UNCONSCIOUS
AFTER BEING STRUCK IN THE HEAD BY A HAILSTONE THE SIZE OF A GOLF BALL)

☐ Raining frogs? (10,000 POINTS FOR ANY BIBLICAL PLAGUE OR SIMILAR
SIGN FROM GOD; MUST BE VALIDATED BY PRIEST, RABBI, OR CREDENTIALED
CLERGY MEMBER)

3) Mishaps

☐ Give yourself three points for each flat tire

☐ Give yourself five points for every mechanical problem that
required a tool

☐ Give yourself ten points for every mechanical problem for
which you fabricated a tool from found items

☐ Give yourself twenty points for every animal bite you sustained
(double points if you had to extract venom from the wound with
a frame pump)

☐ Give yourself 100 points if you were accosted by a gun-wielding
sex-crazed hillbilly and Burt Reynolds had to shoot him with a
crossbow

HOW EPIC WAS MY RIDE RESULTS:

UNDER 100: Not epic

100–105: Minimally epic

106–150: Epic

151–200: Seriously epic

200+: Free Rapha clothes for life

10,000+: You are that Job guy from the Bible

ARE YOU CULTURED?

FOR SOME PEOPLE, riding a bike just means throwing a leg over the saddle and pedaling. For others, it is an act of profound cultural significance; a proclamation to the world; the basis of an identity. So where do you lie on this spectrum? Take this test to find out:

1) In the past 12 months I've participated in the following:

   ☐ A Critical Mass ride (**1 POINT**)

   ☐ A Tweed Ride (**2 POINTS**)

   ☐ A World Naked Bike Ride (**3 POINTS**)

   ☐ A World Naked Bike Ride in which all the participants rode saddle-less bicycles and wore Larry King masks (**4 POINTS**)

2) My idea of competitive cycling is taking part in:

   ☐ An unsanctioned singlespeed race (**1 POINT**)

   ☐ A Films of Jim Jarmusch–themed alleycat (**2 POINTS**)

   ☐ A bicycle polo tournament (**3 POINTS**)

   ☐ A tall bike jousting competition to the death on the Golden Gate Bridge bike path (**4 POINTS**)

3) I am an advocate of:

   [**CHECK ALL THAT APPLY**]

   ☐ Car-free living (**1 POINT**)

   ☐ U-lock justice (**2 POINTS**)

   ☐ Bicycle freeganism (using only previously used discarded bike parts and equipment, including cycling shorts) (**3 POINTS**)

   ☐ Replacing municipal power plants with bicycle generators (by 2025 Portland, Oregon will be powered entirely by bicycles, and a new law will require citizens and visitors alike to spend an hour on a bicycle generator for every two hours they spend inside the city limits) (**4 POINTS**)

4) How many bicycle-themed tattoos do you have?

☐ One or more (1 POINT)

☐ Three or more (2 POINTS)

☐ I have an entire sleeve tattoo depicting the Michael Jackson Memorial Theme Ride of June 25, 2009 in Portland, Oregon and I cry every time I look at it (3 POINTS)

☐ Does wearing a thirty-nine-tooth chainring through my septum and a sixteen-tooth track cog in each nipple count as a tattoo? (4 POINTS)

ARE YOU CULTURED? RESULTS:

0–3 POINTS: You have no culture, you are a barbarian

4–8 POINTS: You're a rank-and-file bike culture member; you wear a soiled cycling cap but you take it off when you get to the office

9–12 POINTS: You live in Portland

13 AND OVER: You are steeped in bike culture, you are a barbarian